# The Story of a House
## H. H. Richardson's *Glessner House*

by John J. Glessner

Glessner House Museum
1800 South Prairie Avenue
Chicago, Illinois

Published by
Glessner House Museum
1800 South Prairie Avenue
Chicago Illinois 60616-1320
312-326-1480
www.glessnerhouse.org

Copyright © 2011
Glessner House Museum
All rights reserved

ISBN: 978-0-615-48327-6

The printing of this publication is made possible
by a generous grant from the
Graham Foundation for Advanced Studies in the Fine Arts

Printing: Chicago Press Corporation

Cover design: Erin Neises

# INTRODUCTION

In 1923, John J. Glessner, then 80 years of age, wrote *The Story of a House*, a loving and personal reminiscence of the house at 1800 South Prairie Avenue in Chicago that he and his wife Frances had called home since 1887. The title comes from a book written in 1874 by the French architect and theorist Eugène-Emmanuel Viollet-le-Duc, a copy of which the Glessners owned.

John Glessner was fully aware of the significance of his home and the architect who designed it. But *The Story of a House* was not written as a scholarly monograph about H. H. Richardson or his impact on American architecture. *The Story of a House* was written by a father for his two children – John George Macbeth Glessner and Frances Glessner Lee. It was intended as an intimate story of the house as a family home, and as a record of its furnishings, its occupants and visitors, and some of the important events that shaped the lives of the family members.

This is the first reprint of *The Story of a House* to include the complete text and all photographs (taken by the prominent architectural photography firm of Kaufman and Fabry). A few small errors have been fixed – these have been indicated by placing the corrected word in [brackets]. Otherwise, the manuscript reads exactly as John Glessner wrote it, his personal style clearly reflected in the elegant prose that transports us back to the era that he knew and was attempting to preserve.

The timing of *The Story of a House* coincided with enormous change that was taking place on and around Prairie Avenue. Just a few months after presenting the story to his children, John Glessner wrote to them stating, in part, "Your Mother and I may have to leave our house 1800 Prairie Ave. after a while – how soon can't be told. The Pullman and McBirney houses on the corners of 18th Street have been torn down and the Henderson house, the Kimball house and the Otis-Jenkins house are high class rooming houses, and nearly all the others are business, though of very satisfactory and unobjectionable kind. In this state of transition of course we cannot tell how soon something may happen to make our place unsatisfactory. We have hoped we could live here as long as we needed a house at all, and perhaps we can, who knows. At any rate we shall not move until we have to." John Glessner wrote *The Story of a House* because he realized that the house itself might soon disappear, and his story would be the only tangible reminder of all it meant to his family.

The Glessners were able to remain in their beloved home until their deaths – Frances Glessner in October 1932 and John Glessner in January 1936. For the next thirty years, the house was occupied first by the Armour Institute and then by the Lithographic Technical Foundation, which set up printing presses in the once elegant rooms. When that company moved to Pittsburgh in the 1960s, demolition seemed imminent. A small group of preservationists, determined to rescue Richardson's masterpiece of urban residential design, banded together and saved the house in 1966. Since that time it has been extensively restored, and descendants have returned most of the original furnishings. Today visitors to Glessner House Museum, now a National Historic Landmark, can experience the home just as John Glessner preserved it in *The Story of a House*.

William Tyre
Executive Director and Curator
Glessner House Museum

# THE · HOUSE · AT ·
## · 1800 · PRAIRIE · AVENUE ·
### · CHICAGO ·

✢ 1886 ✢

· H. H. RICHARDSON · ARCHITECT ·

This story is addressed to my son,
JOHN GEORGE MACBETH GLESSNER,
and my daughter, FRANCES GLESSNER LEE,
for whose pleasure and profit it has been my
pleasure and their mother's to do many things,
and especially to give them a happy home
and a happy childhood, and to fit them for the
responsibilities of living.

*John J. Glessner*
*Frances M. Glessner*

with the regards of
H. H. Richardson

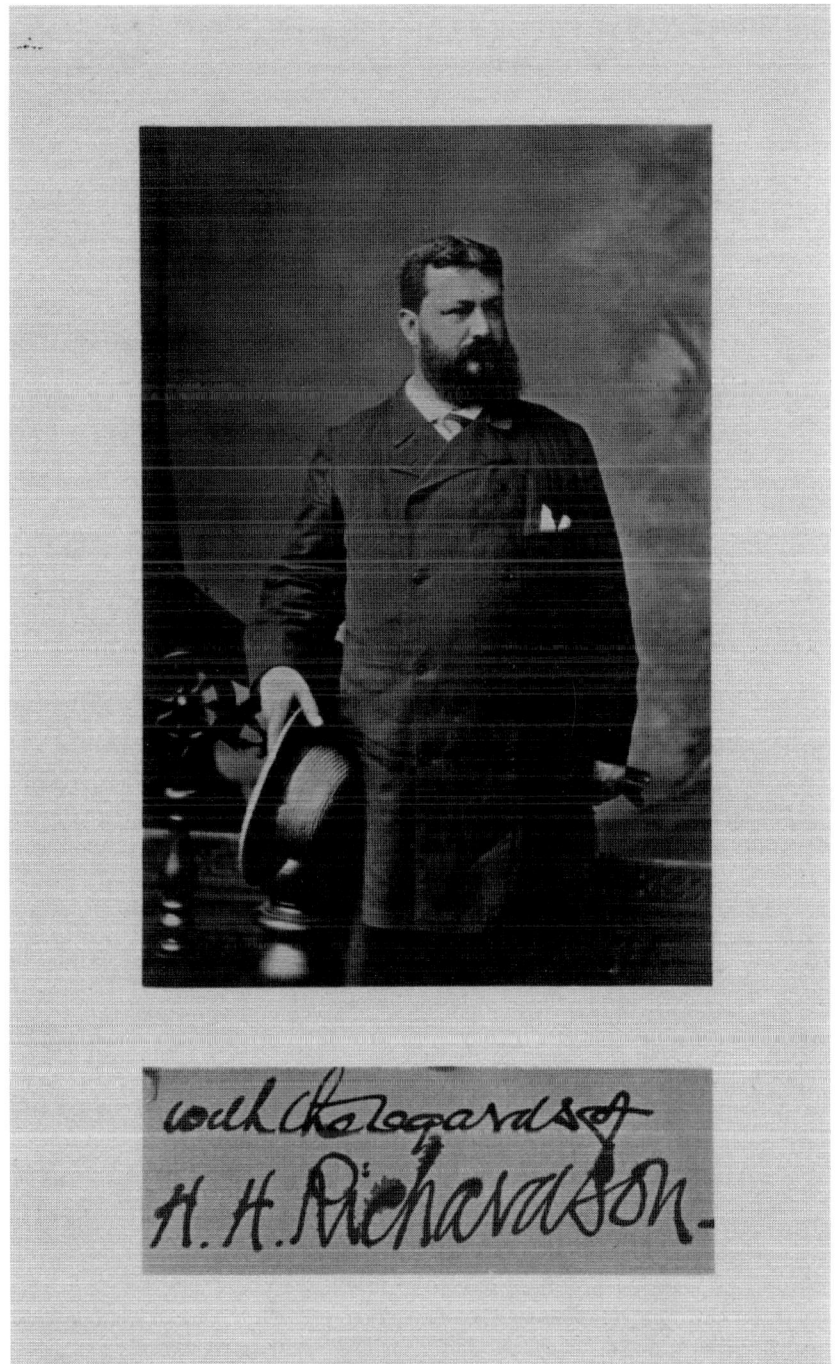

1800 Prairie Avenue
CHICAGO

My dear George and Frances:

Mankind is ever seeking its comforts and to achieve its ideals. The Anglo-Saxon portion of mankind is a home-making, home-loving race. I think the desire is in us all to receive the family home from the past generation and hand it on to the next with possibly some good mark of our own upon it. Rarely can this be accomplished in this land of rapid changes. Families have not held and cannot hold even to the same localities for their homes generation after generation, but we can at least preserve some memory of the old.

Your forbears as far back as I have traced on both sides of the house have made their altar around the family hearthstone, and have tried to keep to its legends when compelled to leave it.

My father's house was very attractive to me. I well remember when he built it, and though I was quite a small boy, the odor of fresh plastering still remains in my nostrils in this long retrospect. And because this recollection persists, I wish to tell you something about our Chicago house at the corner of Prairie Avenue and 18th Street, the home of your childhood. Much of what I write may be well known to you already, part of it may be new, and part may perhaps be irrelevant.

The description of this home may give some indication of how a man of moderate fortune would live in the latter part of the 19th century and the earlier part of the 20th — an average man with a modicum of this world's material possessions, but by no means rich, except in family and friends.

The house was built in 1886. On the morning of June 1st of that year, I sent word from my office to your mother that wheelbarrows, spades and picks had just then been sent to the site of our proposed new home, that digging would begin at one o'clock, and if she would take Frances and nurse, etc. in the carriage, and let George drive my horse and buggy and stop at the office for me, and all of us reach the site soon after twelve o'clock, you two children — George then fourteen and a half years and Frances a little more than eight years old — might throw the first soil from the foundation trenches. And that we did.

Just eighteen months after that to the day, we occupied the completed house. Because of its plan, we were able to move all of our household belongings through the courtyard entrance from the alley, and place them in the house before our neighbors suspected even that [we] were about to move.

These were good, kind friends of ours, these neighbors, the finest and most considerate that any one ever had, and they welcomed us warmly — the Shortalls, the Spauldings, Harveys, Hibbards, Kelloggs, Dexters, Sturges, Walkers, Otises, Pullmans, Armours, Doanes, Keiths, Fields, Hendersons, Clarks, Grays, Allertons, etc., etc., and many others of the same class who came afterwards. Farther south on the Avenue were the Spragues, Bartletts, Hutchinsons, Judahs, Hamills, Lancasters, Gettys, Hugitts, Keeps, Haskells, Henry Blairs, and others, and on the Avenues both east and west were other dear friends.

We slept in this house for the first time on the night of December 1, 1887, and never in the old house after that. The fire on the hearth typified the home, so we carried the living fire from the hearthstone in the old home at Washington and Morgan Streets, and with that started the fire on the new hearth, accompanied by a little ceremony that I don't know if you remember or not; but the old home had been pleasant with many intimate social gatherings — for your mother had ever the genius for generous friendships and hospitality, and the life in the new home must be a continuation of the life so happily lived in the old, and carry on without break its customs and traditions. And so it was with the fire: the old did not go out, the new merely continued its warmth and glow.

The Virginia Creeper vines on the courtyard walls were carried from the old home. All were properly trimmed before replanting except one which was fifty-five feet long, and which when planted was trained its full length. We hardly expected that to grow, but it did, and flourished. The vines on the front were different. Some of our Boston friends knew of Richardson's work here, and when Boston's Commercial Club came to visit ours, June 11, 1887, and I was taking a carriage load of these visitors to Washington Park Club for luncheon and to see some horse racing, several asked if they couldn't be taken past my home, then building, and one — Alpheus Hardy — wanted the privilege of sending Boston ivy to grow over the walls. From plants that he sent came all the vines now on front of the house.

Almost at the beginning — that is, on Sunday December 4, 1887 — we brought our long time familiar and dear friend Prof. David Swing, and other dear and intimate friends, Franklin and Emily MacVeagh and Eames, in to dine and to approve our new habitation. We took them all over the house, upstairs and downstairs and in every room. Before saying good night at starting home, the Professor, then pastor of Chicago's Central (undenominational) Church, said a little prayer of blessing upon the house and its inmates and the friends who might from time to time be gathered within its shelter. And so our new home was started.

Then followed luncheons and teas and receptions and dinners of farewell on the West Side and of welcome on the South.

Here in the new home your mother at once resumed the open house of cheer that had lent charm to the old on Sunday afternoons and evenings, and on holidays for the waifs and strays, so-called, who so often find holidays depressing, young men and women without families or homes in the city. I think there were scores of them before the World's Fair; and at that time and afterwards we tried to make our home a harbor of refuge, not for the casual visitor only but for the University professors and their families, and other fine and gentle folk not yet sufficiently established and with few acquaintances and connections here.

Here, too, she founded the Monday Morning Reading Class that has had continuous existence for more than thirty years. Perhaps this might be called an outgrowth of a smaller company that had irregular meetings for reading and study in the old home, but of this later organization neither illness, nor health, nor pleasure has interrupted the regularity of its weekly meetings through the winters and springs, and its course of study, and, incidentally, its monthly luncheons; and nothing has marred the pleasure of this association together of these cultivated, congenial women. In these three decades there have been few resignations, and no loss of interest, and the meetings are more highly prized now than ever before. The eighty or more members of the class are kind enough to say they find in our library an atmosphere of peace and contentment and charm that has brought genuine affection one for another. The Reading Class has been a great factor for kindly good will, and your mother has been its tutelary genius.

Of course there was something more than the reading. While that went on the ladies' fingers were busy with sewing and other womanly occupation, and when the reading stopped doubtless their tongues grew active in womanly conversation. During the World War the class knitted sweaters, etc., for the soldiers, and since the armistice it has been making sweaters and blankets and garments for convalescents and infants at Cook County Hospital. The amount of this work has been enormous; it has been exceedingly well done, is most gratefully received, and the members of the class have great satisfaction in doing it.

Just a word more about your mother: She had a clean and wholesome and orderly mind, a heart overflowing with love for family and friends and for all in any need. Her remarkable sense of the value of color and fabric and form and arrangement were what made our three homes in Chicago so attractive, and even the small and mean hotel apartments we occupied in the summers for your health, and the various houses in California we rented in the winters for her health, were made homely and pleasant by her deft touches.

A story apropos: A dear old lady once said to me in all seriousness, "Mr. Glessner, you are a very important member of this community; you have a position of great prominence and influence; you get it from your wife and your house." Don't think this disparagement of me. I thought it a real compliment, for I selected the one and I built the other.

This is not the place for any panegyric upon your mother, nor to recount "her many little unremembered acts of kindness and of love:" if I began that I might not complete this story of the house. She was only a slip of a girl when I brought her to Chicago. Chicago was truly the Garden City then, with no apartment houses, few double houses, and only occasional blocks of houses. Even the lowly homes were detached cottages, usually of wood and behind wooden sidewalks, but each with a small plat of ground.

Our first habitation in Chicago, northeast corner of Park Avenue and Page Street, was rented in 1870, and we lived there for five years. The second home, northeast corner of Washington and Morgan Streets, we bought in 1875, and lived there about twelve years. The third, southwest corner of Prairie Avenue and 18th Street, we built in 1886, and have lived there since then.

The Park Avenue house belonged to Judge McAllister, and his family had been its only occupants until we rented it. Here George was born, and afterwards the little brother who died. It was a frame house with a nice but narrow lawn on three sides, and was made attractive within in spite of white marble mantels and similar so-called adornments.

We wished to possess our own home, and bought on Washington Street the house that had been built by Sylvester Lind and occupied by him, then sold to Jacob Beidler, who lived there some years, and sold to me. Both of these families were well known in Chicago at that time. This house was of brick, on the street corner, and the grounds extended for half the block frontage on both streets. Our neighbor, Thomas M. Avery, with a similar lot next east of this, joined with us to remove the dividing fence. His house on the corner of Washington and Sangamon Streets, close to Sangamon, and ours on Washington and Morgan Streets, close to Morgan, left one glorious lawn between, all grass, with bright flowers at the borders, and the only division visible was a big splendid elm tree that stood just inside of my line. At the Morgan Street side was a great pear tree, the largest I had ever seen, and several large maple trees. Again the house was made charming inside. Frances was born there. It really was a cross to leave that place, but the changing neighborhood and the demand for a little more room for you growing children made it necessary.

Then came the present house. Over the thresholds of this has passed a regular procession of teachers for you — in literature, languages, classical and modern, mathematics, chemistry, art, and the whole gamut of the humanities and the practical, considerably beyond the curricula of the High Schools. Whether this plan of education was wise or not may be questioned, but unfortunately George had developed a severe case of hay fever while he was yet less than four years old, and we were advised not to subject him to the nervous strain of a school where he would meet the competition of others. Of this I am sure, that it gave to each of you a great fund of general information, a power of observation and of reasoning, an ability and desire for study, and to be thoroughly proficient in what you might undertake. If ever there was a royal road for that, you had it, whatever its defects may have been in other respects.

The school room, approached from the front door without going through other parts of the house, was a rendezvous for George's friends and teachers alike, for they were all comrades together. Here they had their long, long thoughts of youth, their boyish activities, their fire brigade, their regularly organized telegraph company, presided over, as a labor of love, by Norman Williams, one of the ablest and most astute of lawyers, with wires connecting seven different residences of the members, all centering in this house. Every boy was as free to come and go as George himself, until they dropped it all for the delights and wider associations of college. And then similar activities for Frances and her friends — much studious application, of course, but a plenty of amusement and gentle recreation, and never any shirking. Oh the joys that emanated from that room — No espionage, no punishment, no need for that; no too hard and fast rules, no too rigid disciplinary regulations.

This house was designed by Henry H. Richardson of Brookline, Mass., its construction being under the direct supervision of his assistants and successors, Shepley, Rutan & Coolidge. Shepley and Coolidge were graduates of Harvard and of Massachusetts Institute of Technology. Richardson had a standing offer with the Institute to take into his office for training and employment after their graduation the best three men developed by each class at "Tech," and often said that these two were the ablest he had found. Rutan was his engineer. Shepley was of St. Louis and afterwards married Richardson's daughter: Coolidge was of Boston and married Shepley's sister. Richardson was America's foremost architect at that time, and one of the ablest ever produced here. He would have had a far greater reputation had he lived long enough to do more work. He was building two other residences at the same time he was building ours — Mr. Warder's in Washington and Franklin MacVeagh's here, and of course he had built others. At the time of his death builders were at work upon sixteen important structures of his designing. All together he had had only sixty-four commissions in his entire professional career. From what he told me and what his young men said afterwards, I am convinced that this house of ours is the one of all that he built that he would have liked most to live in himself. It was his last work. Just three weeks before his death, as your mother and I sat with him in his bedroom in his home, — for he was unable to leave it, — he marked in the drawings the places for the lighting fixtures, and turning to me, said: "There, Mr. Glessner, if I were to live five years longer, that is the last thing I would do on your house; my part is finished." On that day, when I felt that I ought not to stay longer and bother him, while he was so ill, his office force begged me to stay — otherwise he would go downstairs to his office, which would be bad for him. On this occasion I saw his bath tub, which had two steps built in it to help him getting in and out. Over his bed he had two large iron rings suspended by straps from the ceiling, that he might grasp these when he got up or turned over. Though he made a trip to Washington after this interview, he did no more work of any kind, and in three weeks from that day he was no more.

Simplicity and proportion were the strongest characteristics of his work. The same style and finish go all though this house, from front to back, whether in show places or in obscure places. The roofs are of red baked tiles, unglazed; the outside walls on the streets are of [Braggville] granite, and all walls are lined with hollow brick, to which the plastering is attached without laths, so there is no place for mice behind the plastering; all bath room walls and floors are of white glazed tiles; the back entrance-corridor and kitchen walls, and the carriage house and stables (now garage) are of white glazed brick. The heating is from the furnace room under the garage, thus avoiding the dust and dirt and noise of coal and ashes in the house, — a hot water system it is, admirable for the time when it was put in.

Either the floors are deadened or the ceilings doubled, or both, so that sounds do not carry through the house; basement and furnace room ceilings are plastered, and all have cement floors.

The courtyard elevation, of common brick of slightly pinkish color, with gray limestone trimmings, is quite as interesting as the street fronts, though in a different way. By special arrangement the same brick were used in the adjoining house, so that all walls of the courtyard are of the same texture and color.

Altogether, the house was as well built in every detail as the architect could suggest or as we knew how to build, and one great cause for satisfaction was that there was absolutely no bill of extra charges. It was completed for the contract price and no more. There were no labor troubles and no disputes with the builders, Norcross Brothers, of Worcester, Mass., or if there were any they were settled by the architects superintendent, [Edward] Cameron, from Richardson's office, who gave his entire attention to this building. George Bosworth succeeded Cameron as superintendent.

The tiles in the mantels of the first-floor bedroom, and of the second guest room are by William De Morgan, with antique Persian tiles in the dining room; fireplaces and andirons are old Colonial and old Continental European, and that in the library is old Scotch, all of them found in junk shops after they had been taken from old buildings; many of the gas and electric fixtures, wall papers, curtains and carpets, except antique rugs, are by William Morris, and have been renewed from the same patterns when renewal was necessary; yellow glass under chipped white glass in the door leading to the courtyard gives a feeling of sunlight in the hall even in cloudy weather.

Mr. Richardson insisted on one or two small extravagances, fine imported marbles in parlor and hall mantels, imported washbowls from the English factories of Meyer-Sniffen, because more generous in size than those to be had here, silver plate on plumbing fixtures, though nickel would have been cheaper and have given less care, but he agreed with Matthew Arnold in bewailing the common "want of fastidiousness and the proneness to mistake nickel for silver," and would have none of that in his work. He was particular about the stair rail and balusters. Of the latter there are [five] different patterns, one of each on each step, all slender, graceful, fine, reproductions from some distinguished old Colonial house — the Longfellow house at Cambridge, if my memory is not at fault — but I distinctly remember that they cost one dollar each.

And then the grille and other iron-work on the front door, and other outside iron-work, he would not have painted, but that must be Bower-Barffed, a process that I think has not come into general use, at least I don't recall seeing it elsewhere, but it has completely protected the iron-work from rust, though exposed to the weather all these years.

He maintained that the windows of a city house were "not to look out of" and should not be large: "You no sooner get them than you shroud them with two thicknesses of window shades, and then add double sets of curtains."

When first built, the house was the subject of much remark by passers-by, because of the narrow windows in its north side along 18th Street, just enough to light the narrow corridors, these critics not realizing that on the south side, looking on the courtyard, Mr. Richardson had put generous windows that let in a flood of sunlight when the sun shines in Chicago.

The house responds: it seems available for almost any social function. Large companies have been entertained in it comfortably and easily; there are two or more entrances or exits to every principal room, so that it is easy to move about, and passages are so planned that servants rarely are in evidence. Music and dramatic readings have been given to hundreds of persons, and receptions to more than four hundred at one time, without any feeling of crush, confusion or heat. Elaborate course dinners have been served in its rooms to more than one hundred guests at a time, the cooking all done in our own kitchen and by our own cook. Twice the full Chicago Orchestra has dined there, and once the Commercial Club.

The kitchen and pantries are on the main or parlor floor, are well lighted, well ventilated, convenient, easily cleaned; and the small dining room adjoining has its table, its little sideboard, its writing desk. The entrance is through the great arch on Eighteenth Street to the small corridor, and thence to these offices. Also there is convenient access down the basement stairs to the school room, so that it is easy to serve company there.

Several times Mr. Thomas brought one third or more of the Orchestra to the house unannounced, as surprise for your mother upon her birthday or some other anniversary, and found it easy to smuggle them into the house without her knowledge. The first she might know of it might be when, sitting at dinner or at a late supper, some soft strains of music floated from the front hall. On the 25th anniversary of our wedding, Mr. Thomas brought the entire orchestra in by the Eighteenth Street door, up the back stairs, and their presence was not known until by his signal they began a delightful concert.

To begin the New Year on Thursday, January 1st, 1903, we gave an afternoon reception to mark your mother's birthday, and with the invitations enclosed Alice's card. At four o'clock lovely strains of music from a double quartet of horns came from the upper hall. The musicians had slipped in through the Eighteenth Street door and up the back stairs with no one the wiser except you two, and you were told that some refreshment might be provided. The men had asked Mr. Thomas to bring them up and give them the privilege of playing for us. Mr. Thomas said that always before he had brought the orchestra — this time the orchestra had brought him. After the quartet there was other music by about thirty men of the orchestra. Mrs. Thomas had brought Horatio Parker, eminent organist and composer, to the reception, and he stayed through the concert.

Three weeks later we gave a dinner to the full orchestra and a few other guests, about one hundred in all. After the dinner the men gave us varied musical and comic stunts, dressing in costume and imitating great artists with great exaggerations, and finally played the metronome movement from Beethoven's Eighth Symphony on pots, pans and dishes — a wonderful and really musical performance.

After all these years the house is full of associations, of course. In this parlor Frances was married, in February, 1898, by Rev. Philip Mowry, then of Pennsylvania, who had performed the same office for your mother and me twenty-eight years before. The rugs were up and the furniture removed, to make smooth the space necessary for the wedding party and the wedding guests. In the former was Alice Hamlin, who had come from her home in Springfield, Ohio. After the ceremony we were happy to announce another wedding in prospect — George's engagement to Alice for the following June.

Twenty-two years later our Golden Wedding celebration was combined with the "coming out" party we gave for Frances Glessner, for her twentieth birthday, December 7, 1920. The two anniversaries came on the same day, but until they were in the house our guests did not know they were celebrating more than Frances' presentation to society. And two years after that we had the pleasure to present another granddaughter to our Chicago friends — Frances Lee, at a gathering of equal size and quality.

Among other things that have helped to make this home what it is is quite a collection of steel engravings of the time that Chas. Summer called their golden age, mostly framed in the somewhat elaborate fashion of the early '80's — the work of our old and valued friend, Isaac Scott. The gathering of the prints consumed a number of years. As in those years the bottom of our purse was easily reached, our choice of what to buy was by elimination. First having one hundred or more plates sent home at a time, usually on some Saturday night in the winter, we would throw out all that did not strongly appeal to us; then go through the remainder a second time, leaving only the choicest; then a third or even a fourth time, until there were left only those we "couldn't live without." It was hard to decide upon that, but we only had so much — or rather only so little that we could spend.

There are a few paintings and drawings, and these by personal friends — Hubert Herkomer, John LaFarge, Albert Herter, Hopkinson Smith, Joseph Linden Smith. Also a monotype, so-called, by A. H. Bicknell, an unusual print, made by smearing a copper plate with printer's ink, and then rubbing off in spots to make the lines and shades of the picture, and then printing after the manner of an etching. In this way each print requires the artist's work as much as a painting. An alcove in the hall was prepared especially for drawings, with cork walls to receive thumb tacks, but used otherwise when the smoky atmosphere compelled putting pictures under glass.

There are some excellent photographs, especially that of Richardson the architect, taken from the oil painting by Herkomer. This portrait was painted under peculiar circumstances. Herkomer had designed for himself a house in [Bushey, England], and was not satisfied with the elevation. Coming to this country with some pictures, he called on Richardson with the request that he be permitted to paint his portrait. "But I haven't money to pay for it," objected Richardson. "You don't need to pay money for it," said Herkomer. "If you will sketch an elevation for my house I'll paint your portrait." And that was all the contract. The elevation was drawn, the portrait was painted. Herkomer showed us the work and promised to etch it and give me the first signed proof, and Richardson agreed to sign also, but alas the great architect died and his widow was unwilling that the portrait be taken to England to be etched. So I lost my double-signed proof; but Mrs. Richardson had the portrait photographed, enlarged by heliotype process, two copies printed and the plate destroyed. This is one of those two copies, and now hangs in the hall. In the painting the coat was a warm light gray, the waistcoat a brilliant primary yellow and the necktie a bright red.

At this time Mr. Richardson weighed three hundred and seventy pounds. There was nothing self-assertive about him, but he would have been marked in any company. Big-minded, big-bodied, big-hearted, he was a dominating personality, large in his own and other arts, in his views of life and of affairs generally. He was doomed to early death, and he knew it, but was not made unhappy either by the fact of his knowledge of it. When I saw this portrait of him, framed, on the sofa in the Richardson library, I was startled: it seemed almost that the man himself was sitting there. The portrait was never quite completed. A close examination of the photograph will show the texture of canvas visible about the eyes and around the mouth.

There are some other photographs and some Braun autotypes of classical subjects.

There are collections of [Gallé] and Venetian and other rare glass, of porcelains and pottery and bronzes, of De Morgan and Minton and other tiles in addition to those in mantels, of jewelry and table and other silverware, especially a George IV tea-set, well authenticated, that bears his crest, first as Prince of Wales, and afterwards as King of England. (Query: Was this the set he gave to Mrs. Fitzherbert?) See note 3d page following. You know, George [IV] really married Mrs. Fitzherbert in 1785, and finally separated from her afterwards that he might marry another and have royal children to perpetuate the dynasty. There is the silver coffee-pot, a part of the official plate of the Spanish Admiral Cerveza's flagship, Christobal Colon, sunk at the battle of Santiago bay on July 3, 1898, and recovered by a sailor of the American fleet, sold by him to a Navy surgeon, and thence to me; there is a [Siamese] punch bowl and ladle that Sir Purdon Clarke of the British Museum said was a museum piece so fine that our Art Institute should keep an eye on it and never let it get away; some interesting old and some more modern furniture, including in the former the mahogany sofa, originally upholstered in haircloth, that was her chief piece of parlor furniture when my mother began her housekeeping, and a beautifully veneered mahogany work-table made by my grandfather Glessner with his own hands, and presented to my mother at her wedding. Some chairs that your mother's mother began her housekeeping with, an old bureau, a family heirloom, once the property of your grandfather Macbeth's mother, etc., etc. The Piano, the action of which was selected by Mr. Stetson of the Steinway firm as the best they could produce, and the case made by Davenport of Boston from design of Francis Bacon, has remained a beautiful and satisfactory instrument all these years.

The furniture in the dining room is from designs by Charles Coolidge; in the drawing room from Francis Bacon's designs — in both cases executed by Davenport; there are some Herter chairs, some Scott bookcases and cabinets and beds (in your mother's bedroom and George's); Francis Bacon's furniture in Frances' room and the main guest room, and in the second guest room a set of typical French furniture bought in Paris. One of the Scott bookcases is the first piece of furniture he designed for us. That was in 1876. We thought then, and still think it beautiful as a single piece.

A small hanging corner cabinet with delicate cameo carving has a peculiar interest: made to hold some sort of funerary remembrance for a deceased member of her family for a lady who either changed her mind or was not quite satisfied and therefore let it be placed in an exhibition where many persons sought to buy it.

In the dining room is an oak silver-chest that George carved himself and had made up while he was a sophomore in college. The carving is especially bold and spirited, and the whole piece is highly prized. Also there is an imported silk embroidered screen of Spanish production, bought in Paris, that shows strong Chinese and Oriental characteristics.

There are a few valuable and interesting bronzes — one of the [33] copies of the head and hands of Abraham Lincoln, made from the original life mask by Leonard W. Volk, and given to the small body of subscribers to the fund to purchase the original mask for presentation to the National Government at Washington. The original mask was made by Sculptor Volk in Chicago in April, 1860, the month before Lincoln's nomination for the Presidency, and the hands were moulded by the same artist in Springfield on the Sunday after the nomination. Lincoln had been whittling with his jackknife and had a piece of broomstick in one hand at the time. There are several small medals, not purchasable but given to us by the artists or subjects, some Japanese vases, and bronze moulds of your mother's hand and of Frances' baby hand. Your mother's hands and arms in the flesh at the time of her marriage were surpassingly beautiful, as lovely as any mortal ever had. Several bronze statuettes are from plaster models for large statues by your mother's cousin J. Q. A. Ward. The bronze busts in the library are copies of antiquities in the Naples museum.

There are several William Morris floor rugs designed and woven especially for this house, and some antique and unusual rugs. There are Morris curtains and portieres, the most important and typical of which had the pattern drawn on the silk by Mr. Morris' own hand, and much, but not all, of the embroidery done by your mother. After these were much worn they were given to the Art Institute here.

The wall papers were also from Morris designs, and when renewed have been continued in exactly the same patterns and colors as when first put on, except in the parlor, where the design and execution in paint on burlaps were by William [Pretyman], a distinguished English artist. At the time the house was finished the green walls of the library were painted blue over yellow after repeated experiments by John Leary, an artist from Davenports, and it has not been necessary to repaint them since.

The table-china and linen and embroideries are unique. I doubt if another such collection of embroideries is to be found anywhere. These are almost exclusively the work of your mother and her sisters, from designs made especially for them by various artists.

An old Leeds pattern pitcher, to hold six quarts, and bearing date 1811, given by the Pottery to Briggs, the Boston dealer, and by him to me, has stood on the sideboard for a good many years, and has often attracted attention for its size and glaze and graceful shape.

There are a number of interesting clocks — English and Dutch and French, and American and Japanese. One tall English clock, now in the second story hall, was bought by my grandfather Laughlin at public venue from his grandfather's estate, and is still an excellent timepiece. Another tall clock, not now in its original case, has been running for more than 125 years, now in the school room. A French clock, a wedding present from my senior partner, Benjamin Warder, and Mrs. Warder, stands on our bedroom mantel and has been running for more than fifty years. Mr. Warder thought a clock the most desirable present that could be given, so constantly in view of the recipient to remind of the giver. There is an old sedan-chair clock, shaped as a great watch. The Japanese clock's hands are stationary — the face revolves.

There are books, several thousand volumes, some of them rare and valuable, collected somewhat at random during our more than fifty years of housekeeping, including many dictionaries and reference works, concordances, etc.

There are household ornaments and much bric-a-brac.

I might call especial attention in the library to a tiny terra cotta bust of Cicero that went through the Great Fire in Chicago in 1871, and still bears its marks, though it was buried in sand at the time; to an antique marble head, said to have been taken from some Roman ruin; to a remarkable Hispano-Moresque bowl; to a fine piece of old Satsuma that was used to illustrate an article in Harper's Magazine many years ago; to a pair of mottled Japanese vases from the Centennial Exposition of 1876, to a Greek amphora, decorated, thought to be a fine specimen; some early Wedgewood, etc. In the hall are two early Roman grain jars of unglazed terra cotta, brought from Civita Vecchia. In the parlor there is an interesting fragment of an antique marble statuette that came from Florence. And there are many, many other things.

We have lived with these things and enjoyed them; they are a part of our lives. We don't realize how many they are and how much a part of us they are until we begin to catalogue them in our minds. We don't know what we should do without them nor what we can do with them. The best we can do now is to make this imperfect record, together with these photographs, to perpetuate or at least suggest the spirit of the home. That home was ever a haven of rest. It was no easy task to make it so, but it was so made and so kept by the untiring and devoted efforts of your mother.

Perhaps you and those who come after you may be interested to look this record over on some rainy day, when lacking better occupation. I would have you realize that it is more a catalogue than a history, and sadly deficient as either or even as a sketch, but it may recall happy experiences of your own youth here and lead in your imagination to pictures of the happy hours your forbears had here.

*Faithfully your father*

*John J. Glessner*

March 1923.

Note:

I find the following letter from John Wells in regard to the silver service that was formerly the property of King George IV. This service consisted of kettle with lamp and stand, teapot and tray, sugar bowl, coffee-pot, lamp and stand, tea caddy, cream ewer, twelve teaspoons and sugar tongs, engraved with monogram, crown, royal arms, and Prince of Wales plumes.

Nov. 18, 1893.

The silver gilt service was made for King George IV in 1792—5, when he was Prince of Wales; and about the year 1825, when he was King of England, he gave it as a marriage gift to the Marchioness of Conyngham, and it afterwards descended to the late Lord Charlemont, who resided near Dublin; and at his death about two years ago his plate was sold in Dublin, and I purchased the service and many other things.

John Wells,
508 Oxford Street,
London, England.

Date marks — 1792 to 1795.

Made by Henry Chawner and
John King, London.

*The Key Note picture, see next page*

# 1800 Prairie Avenue
## CHICAGO

Let me explain why we built our house on this plan, and how we came to select this architect.

 Though I had heard much of Richardson, I didn't go to him first when seeking an architect, for Boston friends had told me that he would undertake only monumental buildings. In New York I saw Stanford White of McKim, [Mead] & White, and also Willie Potter, and engaged the latter to make plans, with the distinct understanding that I might ask others to plan also and should be at liberty to take the one I liked best, paying for the others. When I got home I decided to consult Richardson anyhow, and wrote him what I had heard. His reply was: "I'll plan anything a man wants, from a cathedral to a chicken coop. That's the way I make my living. I am going out to Cincinnati about the Chamber of Commerce, and then to Chicago about Field's wholesale store and will see you there." I told Franklin MacVeagh of this and promptly called on Richardson at Grand Pacific Hotel, as did MacVeagh a few hours later. Then I wrote to Mr. Warder, and he engaged Richardson to plan his house in Washington.

 Richardson asked me what I wanted in a house, and in trying to tell him I suggested that if he would come into my present house I could tell him in half an hour what it would take a day to do elsewhere. He was agreeable, and we got into a carriage at once and went home. On entering he said: "I'll sit on the piano stool if you don't mind. I can't get up easily from one of those easy chairs." He wanted to know what rooms on first and what on second floors, and then: "How will you have them placed?" Oh, no, Mr. Richardson, that would be me planning the house. (Observe my grammar.) I want you to plan it. That's your job. If we don't like it we'll change it. He laughed and made note of the rooms.

 On the library mantel stood a small photograph of a building at Abingdon Abbey. "Do you like that?" Yes. "Well, give it to me: I'll make that the keynote of your house." After his death his office young men sent it back to me with the blot of ink that had been dropped on it while using it for inspiration. Richardson and I drove down to see the lot: your mother couldn't go. He didn't get out of the carriage, but looked at the place attentively and in silence for some minutes, and then blurted out — "Have you courage to build the house without windows on the street front?" And promptly I said Yes, knowing that I could tear up the plan if I didn't like it. Then he added, "I wish I didn't have to go to dinner this evening. I'd give you the plan of your house in the morning." He was to dine at Mr. Field's that night, and with us the next night, and go from our house to the train. While the last course of our dinner was being removed before dessert, he called for pencil and paper, saying: "If you won't ask me how I get into it, I will draw the plan for your house." First making a few marks to get an idea of the scale, he rapidly drew the first floor plan, almost exactly as it was finally decided on. The dessert was strawberry shortcake, for which our cook was famous. He asked for a second piece, with the added remark — "Mrs. Glessner, that's the best pie I ever put in my mouth."

 Stanford White had given me a card to see a house he had just completed in 5th Avenue opposite Central Park for a New Yorker who had large timber interests in the South and who had used only his own woods in the house. There was no furniture in the rooms, and I was struck with the beauty of the eighteen inch wide base-boards and the lower rails of the doors exactly the same height. I wanted mine the same way. Richardson said "No; each baseboard would have to be jointed and glued up; it would cost much more and be no better, and they couldn't be seen anyhow when curtains were hung and furniture in place."

I asked the probable cost of the house, but he couldn't tell, and to my suggestion that I should have to add perhaps twenty-five per cent for extras he said, "Not at all; when I tell you the cost that will be the whole of it." And it was.

When he showed his preliminary sketches the first time and we had expressed hearty approval, he said — "That's for show. Now we'll throw that away and go to work on your real house."

Some months later, when we saw the plans nearly completed one Sunday morning at his office, which was connected with his house at Brookline, your mother said she didn't like part of the second floor. "Well, madam, you don't need to have it that way. What is it you don't like?" The servants' bedrooms haven't any closets. There was one of those flat oval pencils such as carpenters sometimes use lying on the drawing table. He picked that up, drew a broad X over that beautiful drawing, and faster than I can write it, sketched in admirable closets for each room. And that was not changed.

He was the most versatile, interesting, ready, capable and confident of artists, the most genial and agreeable of companions. Everybody was attracted to him at sight. He delighted in difficult problems: among other things, he had a great desire to build a grain elevator in Chicago, and would have made it beautiful. Other architects didn't relish going into a competition with him — "he had such taking ways with the Committee."

Willie Potter, another charming man, came out from New York to explain his plan, and it was a good plan, too. While he was visiting in our house Richardson's plans came by express, but, of course, were not opened — not until after I had put Potter on the train for New York. Incidentally, at the train, I introduced him to Ned Mason, a very brilliant friend of ours, who was going to New York by the same train. Afterwards Mason thanked me heartily for having given him so charming a companion for his journey. When we looked at Richardson's plans that night our minds were made up.

Richardson was an eccentric man. His assistants were devoted to him. The young men who took over his business after his death completed at their own cost every piece of work that was then in the office and turned over to Mrs. Richardson the entire commissions, without any deductions whatever, and the amount was more than $85,000.00.

Richardson's office and house were under the same roof. If he had any important work on hand he would ask some of his assistants to stay at the office and work in the evening, and the first that Mrs. Richardson would know if it might be at five o'clock that he would have one, two, three or a dozen young men stay to dinner. That didn't seem to disconcert her.

The building of the house was an important, absorbing matter to us, and we saw Richardson frequently and intimately at his home. Once he was taking us to drive, and afterwards we were to dine with him at the Country Club at Brookline. Evidently he had sent Mr. Coolidge to make the arrangements, for he came running after us to say — "Mr. Richardson, you can't dine at the Country Club. The London Cricket Club is dining there tonight." The only answer was — "Mr. Coolidge, we will dine at the Country Club tonight." So Coolidge went back. When we drove up to the Club, we were greeted by a band of music, playing English airs, the hosts and servants thinking we were the first of the cricketers. On another visit we had the pleasure of taking first his eldest daughter out to her first dinner party, and afterwards his younger daughter to her first party.

The house he built for the MacVeaghs was beautiful, and beautifully furnished: the parlor, library, dining room from which a large conservatory opened, made up the first floor; the exterior walls of Ohio sandstone, roof of red tiles. The Warder house was beautiful, too, the front of gray Bedford or similar stone, all smoothly cut and therefore more refined than either of the other two, the first floor given up to the reception room, picture gallery and dining room, kitchen in basement, living rooms on second floor and bedrooms on third.  All of these houses had the front doors opening on the street level and the approach to the first floors up a few steps inside the house.

    A few more words about Richardson the man.  He was born in Louisiana of wealthy parents, and in his youth had the schooling and advantages that wealth could give.  He was graduated from Harvard, and then sent abroad to study art and particularly architecture with Viollet-le-Duc and others.  For several years he was in France and Italy.  The Civil War brought bankruptcy and death to his father and compelled Richardson to return home to make his living.  He began in Buffalo.  While in college and afterwards he had gathered a considerable library of rare architectural works, and this he sold for means of livelihood until he could become established.  For his first work he entered an advertised competition for a church at Springfield, Mass.  About the time the plans were to be sent in the Trustees decided not to build.  Richardson thought this was not fair and so, gathering his plans together, he went straight to Springfield, induced the Trustees to hear the competitors and returned in triumph with the commission.  That church stands in State Street — Unitarian.

    Your mother and I sat with him alone one Monday morning in Trinity Church, Boston, talking about many things and looking at Burne Jones' and William Morris' stained glass windows, the latter "with the bough treatment all powdered over with angels."  He said the congregation was proud of the church.  "But they ought not to be.  Think what I could do now."

    Richardson was not yet forty-eight years old when he died.  He left few monuments to his worth and ability.  If genius is the capacity for taking infinite pains he was a great genius, for he took infinite pains with everything he did.  He built, if not for eternity at least for time.  He objected to some stone I had suggested — "that wouldn't last a hundred years."  Nearly all of the residences he built have passed out of the hands of the original owners because of deaths, of changing fortunes or of changes in neighborhoods, and several have been torn down to make room for other buildings, notably the MacVeagh house and the Warder house.  The monumental structures were few, but all were striking.  The latest of these, the County buildings at Pittsburgh, he considered his best.  All of his work was stamped with his individuality.  It had great influence upon contemporary architecture and that which immediately followed, and his early death was a distinct loss to this country.

*1800 Prairie Avenue*

*Driveway door*

*Driveway Door*

*18th Street Elevation*

*18th Street Arch*

*18th Street Gable*

*West Gable 18th Street*

*Entrance Hall Stairs*

*Entrance Hall looking east*

*Entrance Hall looking into School room*

*School room - east & south sides*

*School room, west & north sides, entrance hall through the door*

*Main Hall, north end*

*Main Hall, Richardson's Portrait over hall seat*

*Morris Rug designed & woven for this hall*

*Main Hall, south end showing corridor to bedroom*

*Principal Bedroom, north side*

*Principal Bedroom, east side*

*Principal Bedroom, south side, dressing rooms beyond*

*Library through door from main hall*

*Library, east side, windows look on Prairie Avenue*

*Library, north side*

*Library, west & north sides*

*Library, west & south sides*

*Parlor through hall door*

*Parlor, west side, Dining room showing through the door*

*Parlor, east side, main hall through the doors*

*Parlor, looking from south window at circular tower*

*Dining room, west wall & part of bay*

*Dining room, west & north sides*

*Kitchen west wall*

*Upper Hall, north & west sides*

*Upper Hall, west side, The Scott bookcase mentioned on page 14*

*Upper Hall, old clock see page 15 of type writing*

*Frances' Bedroom, east & south sides*

*Frances' Bedroom, west & north sides   Book cases not here originally*

*George's Bedroom, west & south sides*

*George's Bedroom, north & east sides*

*Corner Guest room, south & west sides   Upper hall shows through the door*

*Corner Guest room, window opens on 18th street*

*Second Guest room, north & east sides*

*From the Courtyard, showing dining room bay, hall bay, circular tower & driveway to Prairie Avenue*

*From the Courtyard, showing parlor, hall, & south corridor windows*

*From the courtyard, showing circular tower*

*From the courtyard, showing circular tower & driveway*

*From the Courtyard looking west, showing kitchen on the right garage etc in front*

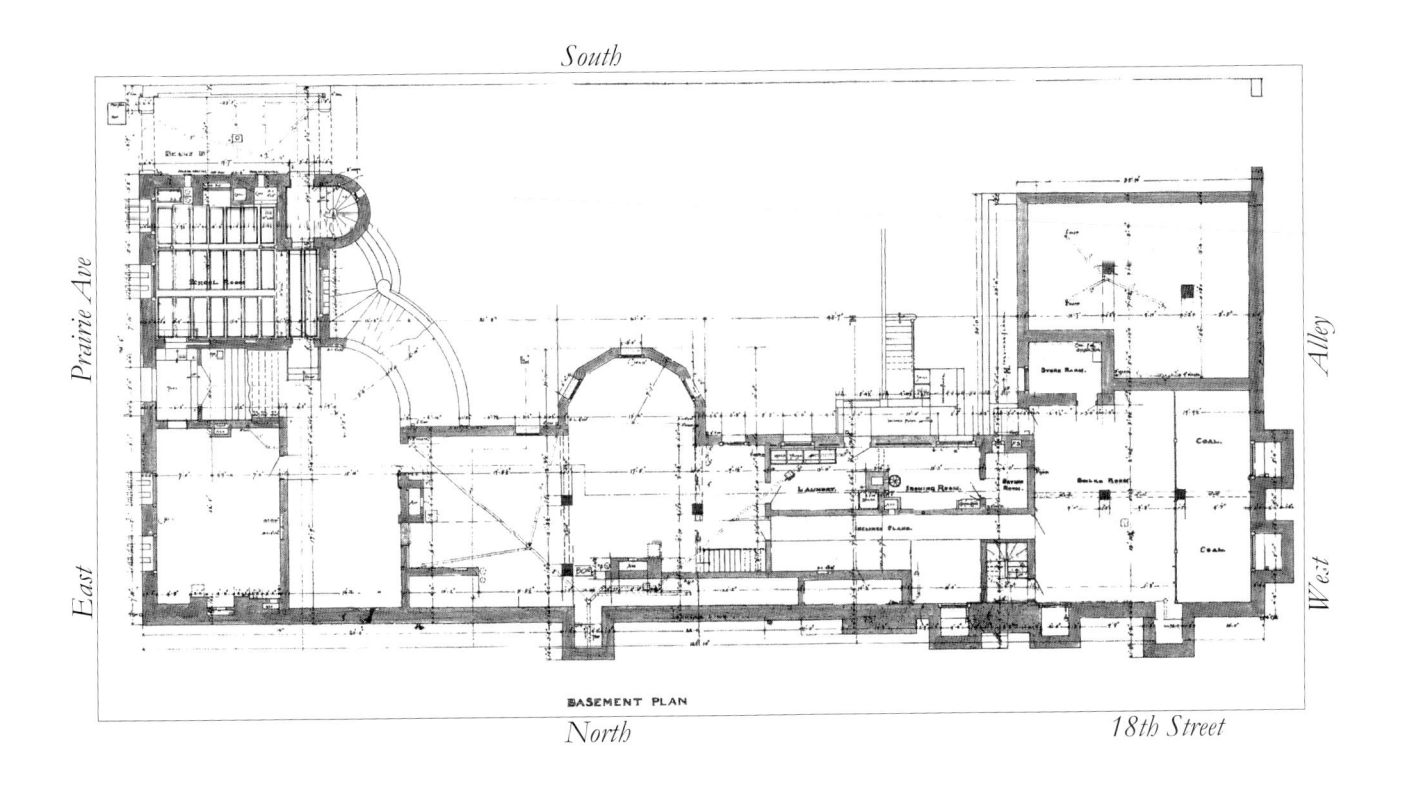

The one continuous stairway from the bottom to the top of the house fills the small circular tower and made convenient access from our sleeping rooms to yours when you were small. The five other stairways go only from one floor to the next and are neither continuous nor one over another, so that each was placed where most convenient for use and to avoid deep well holes.

The street floor contains the school room, with its floor eighteen inches (three steps) below the regular basement floor, the laundry, some storage rooms, the furnace room with floor six feet below basement, approached by an inclined plane.

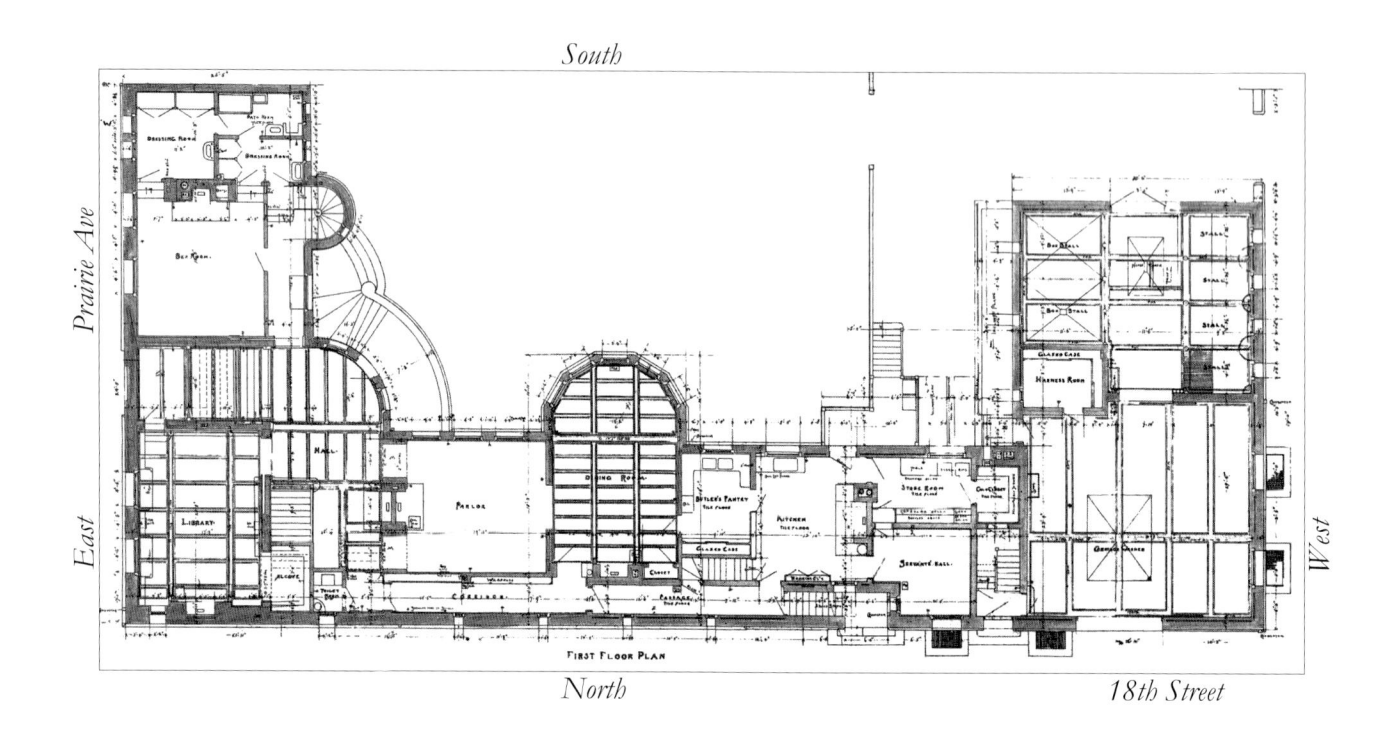

The first floor contains the principal bedroom, the main hall, library, parlor, dining room, each room being about 18 ft. x 25 ft. in dimensions, kitchen, etc.; the second floor is all bedrooms, and the third has the butler's room, a small sewing room, and storage.

There are ten open fire-places in the house, all with unusually broad and high mantels, admirably proportioned and attractive.

Though it is all under the same roof, there is no connection between the house and the garage and its apartments, but both have direct access to the furnace room.

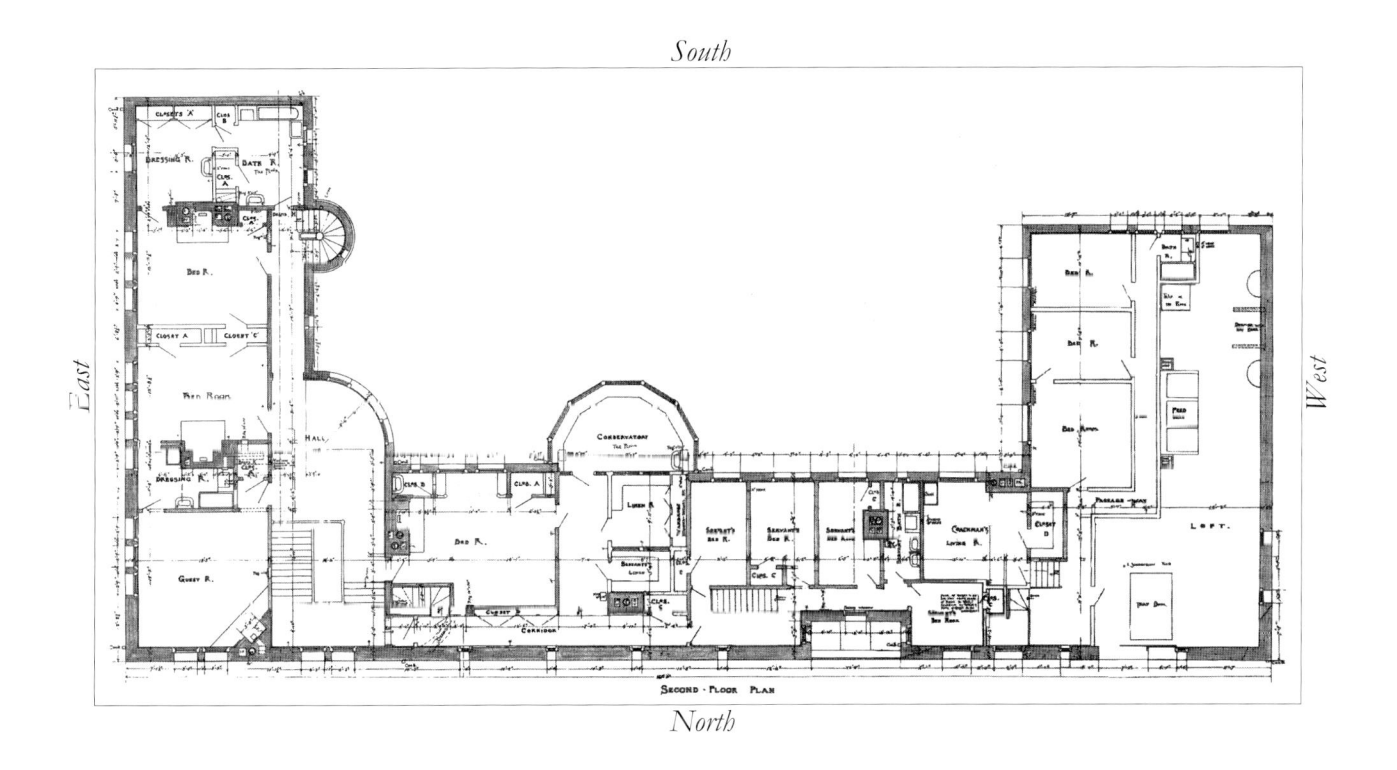

The defects of the house are: there should be a lavatory adjoining the school room, a bath room connecting with the second guest room, another with the butler's room. From the butler's pantry to the front door requires a good many steps, but that could not be avoided. If I were building again I would try to make the small dining room a little wider at the expense of the kitchen pantry.

At first several of the flues did not draw well, a fault not uncommon in Richardson's work, but they were easily corrected.

Remarks about the house at 1800 Prairie Avenue, taken from Mrs. Glessner's diary.

Pullman, Henderson, Wheeler, etc. wrote a letter to John, protesting against his house being set out farther than theirs, and against the general character of the building, basing all of their objections upon hearsay. Before they sent the letter, Mr. Bartlett and Mr. Birch advised them not to send it. Both of these men, and Otho Sprague, told John about it.

Mrs. Dexter wrote me a letter, giving her views and objections. These, and many remarks besides, were all made before our house was commenced.

Mrs. Arthur Caton asked for an introduction to me at a reception, left the tea which she was pouring, crossed the room, etc.

Professor Swing encouraged me, and said it would come out all right and be beautiful.

Frederick Law Olmsted said it was the most beautiful house that had ever been put upon paper.

When we were looking at the house the first time after we came home, we heard one lady say to another in passing, "There is not a single pretty thing about it."

"There are no windows in the first floor of the house," has been said and printed many times.

"The most singular house."   Mrs. Kelley.

"A peculiar structure. Is it a private residence?" An old man wandering through the house one day without permission.

"How do you get into it?"   Many people.

"Have you light enough?"   Many people.

"Is the driveway high enough?"   Many people.

"How do you see in the street?"   Many people.

"A very large house."   No. 1.

"I presume your house will be very elaborate on the inside." No. "Where is the expense, then? Every one says it is the most costly house ever built here."   Mrs. Hall.

"Have you much stained glass?"

"Have you a mosaic vestibule?"

"Your house would look better in a large lot."   Charles Hutchinson.

"Your house has beautiful lines: we have learned to love it."   Mrs. Harvey.

"I like it.  I think it's the oddest thing I ever saw.  I like it because it is different from other people's." Mrs. Doane and many others.

"It takes courage to build a house like that."   Many people.

"The arch is the most graceful I have ever seen."   Many persons.

This and "It is my ideal."   Flora Johnson.

"I should like to live in it."   Wirt Dexter.

"Do you get the sun in your court?"   Many.

"What a pity you did not buy the next lot."   Many.

"More people will have to hedge on that house."   Dr. Dudley.

"I knew Richardson and know the Glessners, and am willing to wait for the house to be finished before giving an opinion, and am sure to be pleased with the result."   General McClurg.

"I am one of the approvers.  I think it is beautiful."   Professor Swing.

"You are going to have a nice house."   Mr. Bliss.

"I never saw a house that would compare with it."   Mrs. Ellen Mitchell.

"It looks like an old jail," a lady said to Mrs. Enoch Root, who replied, "I only hope I shall be arrested and put in it, when it is finished."

"If I build a house I should try to do what you have, build a novelty."   Will Glessner.

"It is elegant.  It is magnificent."   George Glessner.

"A man asked me why the neighbors did not form a syndicate to buy Mr. Glessner's lot and prevent his building such a looking thing," said Mr. Hibbard, "and I told him we liked it to be different; we like novelties in architecture."

"It is the best bit of architecture in America."   Mr. Badger.

"It will not be long before it is known all over the country as the best house in the city." Mr. Ricker.

"The queerest looking house I ever saw."   Almost every one.

"The best house in that street."   An Englishman.

"I don't like it."   Many.

"It expresses an idea."   Mr. Boyeson.   "I don't like the idea."   Mr. Page.

"The most interesting house I ever saw."   Many.

"It looks as though the most interesting people in the world lived in it."   Miss Howe.

"When will you get in it?"   Every one.

"I go by your house very often, to enjoy it; it is so beautiful."   Mrs. Baldwin.

"You have astonished every one with your strange house."   Mrs. Jewett.

"I want to see that house."   Abby Sage Richardson of New York.

"Such large rooms."   Mrs. Dent.

"I don't like it, and wish it was not there."   George M. Pullman.

"Just the sort of house I should build if I could."   Dr. Adams.

"That house is coming out all right.  I have kept still and now can have the laugh on them." Marshall Field.

"It looks like a fort."   Many.

"What church is this?"   The passer-by.

"The apartment house on the corner of 18th and Prairie Avenue."   Newspaper.

"It is very imposing."   Miss Monroe.

"The Glessner house is full of egregious blunders. They would ask and would take no advice, and had never seen any good houses anyway."   Mrs. Warder.

"Is this an apartment house?"   A visitor.

"It is in no respect what I should want."   Mr. Warder.

"Mr. Richardson planned this house, I believe." "Yes," Mr. Cameron replied to a woman who with two gentlemen was going through the house. "He died, I believe." "Yes." "Well, this was enough to kill him."

"I would just as soon criticize Shakespeare," a man said later the same day.

"I shall flee to your fort for protection in case of war."   Mrs. Elbridge Keith.

"It is like themselves: plain and substantial without, and a sweet and homelike spirit within." Canon Knowles.

"What kind of a person is Mrs. Glessner?" "She is every inch a lady, without bangs or frizzes." Canon Knowles.

"It is queer."    Mr. Lewis.

"Your house looks better; it grows on me."    Mr. Lewis, later.

"You should be considered public benefactors for building it."    Mr. Kretschmar.

"If I were building, that is the sort of house I should try to build."    Dr. Mitchell.

"A lady told me it was the most beautiful house she had ever seen."    Mrs. Schmahl.

"A very interesting house."    Remark No. 1.

"I took another look at our friend's house today. I like it."    No. 2.

"I can't get through the day without passing that house once. I like it the best of any house I have ever seen."    No. 3 Alice Swandale's friend.

"I went through your house with a friend. I never saw a house with such capabilities for furnishing; but difficult to furnish."    Mrs. Kretschmar.

"I went through your house and approve it in every way, the only possible criticism being it should have fifteen more feet to the south, that it might stand alone and not be spoiled by coming in contact with Mr. Keith's."    John D. Carson.

"I enjoy your house exceedingly. It is like a breath from a foreign land. I go all around it often." Mrs. India Kirtland.

"I don't know what makes it so peculiar, but it must be the small windows."    Mrs. Swan.

"I go by it every day."    Mrs. Frank.

"I like it exceedingly. It is a beautiful home."    Mrs. Milward Adams.

"A beautiful house and home."    Mrs. John Ela.

"I like it exceedingly."    Mr. Robertson, the architect, of New York.    "It will be comfortable to live in."

"It is like a house in St. Augustine. I wonder if Mr. Richardson didn't tell you it was copied from that."    General Thompson.

"Shall you have vegetation in the court or cover it with glass?"   General Thompson.

Mr. McKim, of McKim, [Mead] & White, architects, went through the house with Mr. Earl, and said in most emphatic terms it was the best thing in every respect that he had ever seen. He examined each room in the whole building, cellar and all, in detail."

"I think it is an awful homely house on the outside."   Mr. Montague.   "I liked it better the second time I saw it. On the inside it is the most beautiful house I ever saw."

"I never saw so splendid a house. On the inside it is perfect. Why didn't you make the front door as good as your side door?"   Virginia Johnson Montague.

"I hear you have no lake view."   Dr. Chambers of New York.

Mr. Sayles of Providence did not like the house, and said we would regret building one so large. His own house was nothing but a tomb. Mattie Sayles thought it the most artistic, beautiful house she had ever seen. Miss Davis, her companion, thought so too.

"I don't know what I have ever done to have that thing staring me in the face every time I go out of my door."   Mr. Pullman.

"What is it? a house?"   Two men to their driver, in a passing carriage.

"It is an old country house, the kind one sees abroad, beautiful in every way. People think that it is because I like George so much that I like the house. George is a part of my life."   Mrs. Schmahl, Teacher of German.

The house was much talked of at luncheon at Chicago Club at what was called "Millionaires' table," and some of my friends, especially Franklin MacVeagh and John Crerar, delighted to stir Pullman to criticism, until Albert Sprague said one day, "Frank, you must not let this go on any longer. We may produce some ill feeling between Glessner and Pullman, and they both are our friends." "All right, Albert, I'll fix it tomorrow." And so when the subject came up again Pullman criticized, and ended with, "Ninety-eight men out of a hundred would agree with me." And MacVeagh, "Well, George, that's just about the proportion of men who don't know anything about architecture." The discussions ceased.

Later Crerar told me that Pullman complained of the rough brick wall of the Coleman house across 18th Street from him and across Prairie from me, but I was either too dense to understand he was trying to draw from me some expression against Pullman or too shrewd to be caught in such trap, for I said never a word. The Coleman wall could not be seen after the next house (Kimball's) was built.

Mr. Pullman got over his dislike when my house was finished. He used often to ask me to ride horseback with him, but my horse didn't behave well in company and we rode together only two or three times; besides, the back of a restive horse isn't an ideal place from which to carry on conversation.

Both Mr. McKim and Mr. Robertson were great architects, second at this time only to Mr. Richardson. These three men were too big for professional jealousies, and were warm personal friends. Mr. Robertson was then planning Governor Bushnell's fine house in High Street, Springfield, Ohio.

I might add that many of the lesser architects asked the privilege to go through our house to gain ideas or inspiration for their own work.

*The Warder House, 1515 K Street, Washington DC*

*Library in the Warder house*

*The MacVeagh House, Lake Shore Drive & Schiller Street*

*Governor Bushnell's House, East High Street, Springfield Ohio*
*Robert H. Robertson, Architect*

*In Summer - see vines*

*In Summer - see vines*

*In Summer - see vines*

*In Summer - driveway door open*

*Court yard in Summer*

*Court yard in Summer*

*Court yard in Summer*